USER'S GUIDE

a year-by-year series for teachers in primary schools

Dorothy Taylor

SCHOTT
EDUCATIONAL
PUBLICATIONS

KEY STAGE 1   Programme of Study

Pupils' understanding and enjoyment of music should be developed through activities which bring together requirements from PERFORMING and COMPOSING, and LISTENING and APPRAISING wherever possible.

1. Pupils should be given opportunities to:
a use sounds and respond to music individually, in pairs, in groups and as a class;
b make appropriate use of IT to record sounds.

2. When performing, composing, listening and appraising, pupils should be taught to listen with concentration, exploring, internalising, *eg hearing in their heads*, and recognising the musical elements of:

a PITCH - high / low

3. The repertoire chosen for performing and listening should extend pupil's musical experience and knowledge, and develop their appreciation of the richness of our diverse cultural heritage. It should include music in a variety of styles:

a from different times and cultures;

b by well known composers and performers, past and present.

b DURATION - long / short; pulse or beat; rhythm;
c DYNAMICS - loud / quiet / silence;
d TEMPO - fast / slow;
e TIMBRE - quality of sound
eg tinkling, rattling, smooth, ringing;
f TEXTURE - several sounds played or sung at the same time / one sound played on its own;
and the use of the above within
g STRUCTURE - different sections, *eg beginning middle, end;* repetition, *eg repeated patterns, melody, rhythm*

4.
Pupils should be given opportunities to:
a control sounds made by the voice and a range of tuned and untuned instruments

b perform with others, and develop awareness of audience, venue and occasion;

c compose in response to a variety of stimuli, and explore a range of resources, *eg voices, instruments sounds from the environment*

d communicate musical ideas to others;

e listen to, and develop understanding of, music from different times and places, applying knowledge to their own work;

f respond to, evaluate, live performances and recorded music, including their own and others' compositions and performances

PERFORMING and COMPOSING
5. Pupils should be taught to:
a sing songs from memory, developing control of breathing, dynamics, rhythm and pitch
b play simple pieces and accompaniments, and perform short musical patterns by ear and from symbols;

c sing unison songs and play pieces, developing awareness of other performers;
d rehearse and share their music making;

e improvise musical patterns, eg invent and change patterns whilst playing and singing;
f explore, create, select and organise sounds in simple structures

g use sounds to create musical effects, *eg to suggest a machine or a walk through a forest;*
h record their compositions using symbols, where appropriate.

LISTENING and APPRAISING
6. Pupils should be taught to:
a recognise how sounds can be made in different ways, *eg by blowing, plucking, shaking, vocalising;*
b recognise how sounds are used in music to achieve particular effects, *eg to soothe, to excite;*
c recognise that music comes from different times and places;

d respond to musical elements, and the changing character and mood of a piece of music by means of dance or other suitable forms of expression;
e describe in simple terms the sounds they have made, listened to, performed, composed or heard, including everyday sounds.

TARGETING MUSIC

KEY STAGE 1 User's Guide

The *Targeting Music* books have been planned to link closely to the National Curriculum Programme of Study, and teachers have been promised stability until at least 2000 with regard to specified curriculum content. The charts in this booklet should therefore provide a secure framework against which to check your detailed planning - short, medium and long term.

There is a *Targeting Music* book for each year, starting with Reception, and a CD supplementing the first three books. The charts in this booklet show, chapter by chapter, song by song, which areas of the National Curriculum (England) are covered.

The charts make apparent the particular emphases in the Reception (pre Key Stage 1) book, and the way coverage then spreads across all strands as the series progresses. One can also see at a glance how the various lessons organize learning for the children as individuals, in pairs, in groups and as a whole classes.

The charts will serve as a checklist for **coverage**, to help fulfilment of legal requirements. They will also help you to maintain **balance** in your curriculum provision, and to plan for **progression**.

The authors do not claim that *Targeting Music* addresses every detail of the National Curriculum. However, as 'musical models' the series will be further supported by this booklet of charts - and further helped to guide this most fundamental stage of children's musical education.

The publishers wish to thank the copyright owner for permission to reproduce the Programme of Study for Key Stage 1 from MUSIC IN THE NATIONAL CURRICULUM. Crown copyright is reproduced with the permission of the Controller of HMSO.

YEAR TWO

TARGETING MUSIC

	1 (a)				1 (b)	2 (a)	2 (b)	2 (c)	2 (d)	2 (e)
	1 Individuals	**2** In Pairs	**G** In Groups	**C** As a Class	**b**	**a**	**b**	**c**	**d**	**e**
MODULE 1 - Dynamics				◆						
1. Lovely things	◆			◆			◆			
2. Lovely things (development)	◆		◆				◆			
3. The animal kingdom			◆	◆		◆	◆			◆
4. I can sing quietly			◆	◆			◆		◆	◆
5. In the distance	◆			◆			◆			
6. The wheel never stops	◆	◆	◆	◆			◆			
MODULE 2 - Pitch				◆						
1. The up and down song	◆					◆				
2. Little red bird: a Manx lullaby				◆		◆	◆			◆
3. Little red bird (development)	◆		◆	◆		◆				
4. Happy Divali	◆			◆		◆				
5. Chanukkah candles	◆		◆	◆		◆				
6. Gentle donkey	◆			◆		◆				
MODULE 3 - Rhythm				◆						
1. Oliver Twist	◆		◆				◆		◆	
2. Oliver Twist (development)			◆	◆			◆			
3. I'm a magician	◆			◆			◆			
4. Are you sleeping	◆		◆	◆			◆			
5. Sur le pont d'Avignon				◆			◆			
6. Poems and stories as stimuli for composing			◆	◆			◆			
MODULE 4 - Timbre or tone quality				◆						
1. Lots of different sounds	◆									◆
2. Lots of different sounds (development)			◆	◆						◆
3. Ting, tap, crash			◆	◆						◆
4. Sound discoveries			◆	◆						
5. Sounds from across the world			◆	◆						◆
6. Moving mode			◆	◆						
MODULE 5 - Texture				◆						
1 Sounds around	◆	◆	◆				◆			◆
2. Sound layers			◆	◆			◆			
3. Togetherness	◆	◆		◆						◆
4. Building sounds	◆	◆		◆						
5. Turn the glasses over	◆	◆		◆			◆			
6. Rainbow colours	◆		◆	◆						
MODULE 6 - Structure				◆						
1. Who's that yonder	◆	◆	◆			◆				
2. Hush little baby			◆	◆						
3. John Brown's body			◆	◆						
4. A ram sam sam	◆	◆	◆	◆						
5. More rounds			◆	◆						
6. Wedding day at Troldhaugen										

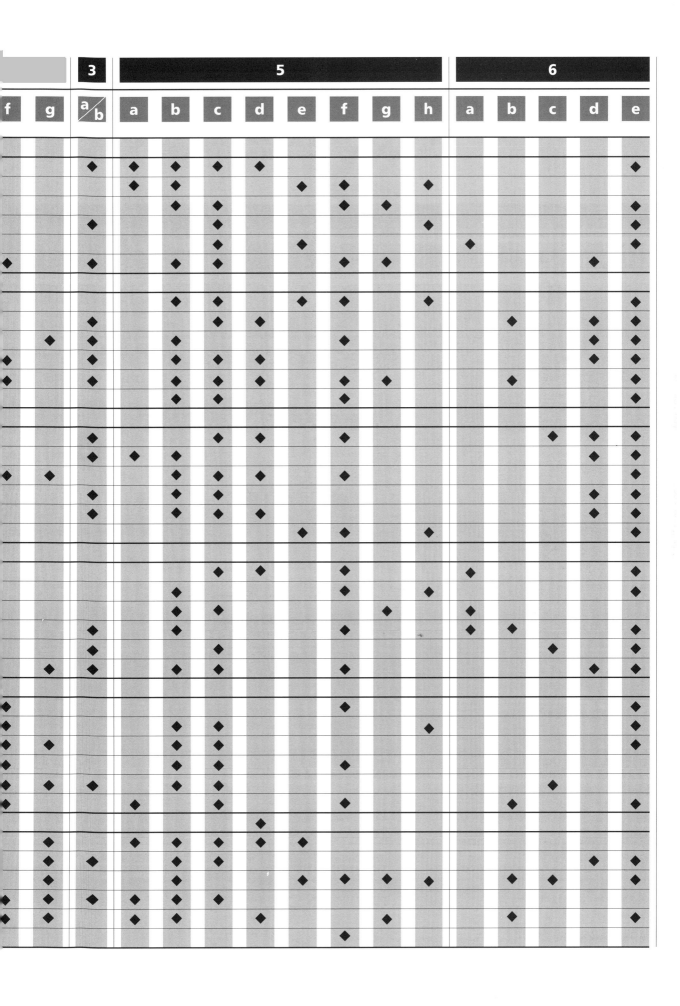

TARGETING MUSIC

A year-by-year series for teachers in primary schools

A major new series of books initiated by Dorothy Taylor, addressing the needs of the music curriculum in primary education. Assembled for use by teachers without specialist training but wishing to use their own abilities – however modest, as singers or players – to deliver a musically rich diet to classes in their charge.

Key Stage 1 User's Guide

Inside this booklet you will find charts to help you plot usage of the *Targeting Music* books and CD against coverage of the National Curriculum (England)

Reception Year (age 4-5) ED 12445

Dorothy Taylor

This is the first book in the series. With plentiful guidance for the teacher, it lays a foundation of musical experience through integrated activities and a repertoire of songs and singing games. It aims throughout to encourage a feeling for music and to cultivate a sensitive listening ear.

Year 1 (age 5-6) ED 12449

Dorothy Taylor

Building on the book for Reception Year, here are 38 model lessons approaching music through the fundamental musical experiences: exploring and creating, listening and performing. The encouragement of active listening is central.

Year 2 (age 6-7) ED 12456

Dorothy Taylor and Jo Brockis

In this the third book of the series, the programme for Year 2 develops more sustained and challenging learning experiences. Attuned to the National Curriculum, content is organised through the musical elements: sound, silence, dynamics, rhythm, pitch, timbre, texture and structure.

A CD - **ED 12483** is available to supplement the first three *Targeting Music* books (covering the infant years). It contains all of the original songs, and also short extracts covering most of the listening suggestions in the text.

Dorothy Taylor is one of our foremost educators. She has extensive teaching experience in primary schools, and compiled the *Learning with Traditional Rhymes* series for Ladybird Books. She has taught at the University of London Institute of Education, and continues to lecture and write extensively. Latterly she has worked as a music adviser and inspector for Essex Local Education Authority.

Jo Brockis is Adviser for Music with the Essex Development and Advisory Service. She has taught in both primary and secondary schools, and has considerable experience in music advisory work for primary schools.

SCHOTT

48 Great Marlborough Street, London W1V 2BN
Tel: (0171) 437 1246 Fax: (0171) 437 0263

Marketing/Sales Department: Brunswick Road, Ashford, Kent TN23 1DX
Tel: (01233) 628987 Fax: (01233) 610232

Targeting
Music

Year 1

Dorothy Taylor

Illustrated by John Minnion

SCHOTT
EDUCATIONAL
PUBLICATIONS

The author and publisher would like to thank Peter Nickol for
his invaluable assistance in preparing this project for publication

British Library Cataloguing-in-Publication Data.
A catalogue record of this book is available from the British Library

ED 12449
ISBN 0 946535 27 2

Designed and typeset by Geoffrey & Marion Wadsley
Music set by Jack Thompson
Cover design by John Minnion

The publishers should like to express their gratitude to the following for permission
to reproduce copyright material:
David Higham Associates for 'Cats' by Eleanor Farjeon, from *The Children's Bells*
Aileen Fisher for 'My puppy' by Aileen Fisher
Laura Cecil Agency for 'Beech leaves', © James Reeves from *Complete poems for
Children* (Heinemann), reprinted by permission of the James Reeves Estate

Every effort has been made to contact copyright holders, particularly in the case of
'The band in the park' by Paul Edmonds. If any right has been omitted, the publishers
offer their apologies and will be pleased to rectify the omission in subsequent
printings.

Contents

Each **odd-numbered** lesson is a **lead lesson**.

Each **even-numbered** lesson is a **development lesson**, using the same song.

Introduction

The repertoire of action songs, rhymes and games in this book provides both familiar and new material – traditional rhymes and new songs. Thirty-eight model lessons are built on these materials, and these are designed to enable teachers to develop sustained listening, performing and composing activities with their classes. While the reception teacher is encouraging children to have a feeling for the overall rhythmic flow of music, in Year 1 more refinement is taking place. Children are becoming more confident in their ability to master singing and playing, and are fast developing their motor skills.

In this book, therefore, the principal aims are that children should be enabled to:
- experience listening, performing and composing music;
- broaden their repertoire of songs, action rhymes and singing games;
- develop and refine their musical skills;
- continue to develop their sensitivity to music through understanding, performing and talking about music.

This is a stage at which children are able to confidently pursue structured learning opportunities. Whatever the focus of an activity, the establishing and maintaining of pleasurable musical experience is our central concern.

As a teacher and artist, you remain an important role model as children continue to learn through imitation and exploration.

The organization of the book

Although there is no need for strict adherence to the order of lessons, there is a sense of progression through the book, broadly from familiar action songs and rhymes through to more complex songs with opportunities for more sustained activities.

Lessons are paired in 'lead' and 'development' lessons – though no hard and fast rule is given about the length of time needed, as every musical encounter presents many possibilities for further development. In teacher-directed activities, it should be stressed that frequent short, concentrated sessions are better for young children than less frequent, longer periods.

Most lessons are spread over a double page, and each pair of lessons starts with a song. The vocal line is presented either unaccompanied or with piano accompaniment. There are chord symbols for guitar or autoharp, which do not necessarily correspond to the harmonic progression in the piano accompaniment.

A commentary running down the margins provides an aide-memoire to musical learning, general learning and cross-curricular links. The suggestions for assessment are intended to be interwoven into the lesson as part of the style of teaching and learning.

Always remember that although this is a stage at which children are being introduced to structured learning processes, our fundamental purpose is still to establish pleasurable musical experiences.

Listening and responding

Listening is central to all musical activity. Young children need constant opportunities to listen and actively respond to music:
- spontaneously and freely in their own way
- through directed activities

They will find opportunities for active and reflective response throughout this book. For example:
- various actions found in finger rhymes and action songs
- locomotor movements (walking, jogging, hopping, etc.)
- listening to their inner musical memory (*Mandy stands so big and tall*)
- listening to another part for timing (*Who made the pie?*)
- listening, drawing, discussing (*Jack Frost*)

Exploring and improvising

To explore and to improvise are natural human tendencies – but the freedom they imply is based on accomplishment gained from absorbing and practising. Young children deserve a musical diet rich with worthwhile material and learning experiences. At the same time they need opportunities to play, explore and practise, and to re-work, make and shape musical material in structured and unstructured settings.

The lessons here include opportunities to:
- suggest different actions for marking the pulse (*The bear went over the mountain*)
- explore sounds and instrumental colour
- respond individually in movement
- try out different instruments to create an effect (*Stars*)
- explore a variety of tasks in a sound or music corner
- investigate, explore, compare different sound sources
- extend classwork
- experiment with vocal sounds (*Incy Wincy Spider*)
- explore and compose (*Who made the pie?*)
- explore instrumental tone colour in small groups (*Little wind*)

Using the voice

Along with the body our voice is the first instrument to be used in a variety of ways: to build musicianship (inner hearing), to chant, to sing in different styles and to use as a sound-source for 'instrumental' colour.

Development varies greatly in young children, depending on prior experience and their growing ability to locate their voices physically and match sounds. Never force this.

The majority of young children sing within a range of five to six notes. The repertoire here is predominantly in this range, although there are several items where the range is wider – especially when a high note is used as an expressive device or feature. Adaptations can be made, and in other cases the aim will be to grasp the feeling and the rhythmic quality of the song, rather than place undue emphasis on accurate pitch.

Young children learn much by imitating good musical models – sensitivity to mood, accurate pitch, good diction and phrasing. To improve children's singing dramatically, concentrate on good, even exaggerated, diction. In formal singing activities, such as assemblies and performances, posture helps too. Children sing well when they stand rather than sit, legs firm and slightly apart, arms loosely at the side, so that their breath can be taken in and contained, supportively, in the lower part of the rib cage. Chins should never be raised, for this constricts rather than opens the throat.

Within the range of materials and suggestions offered, there are many ways to use the voice, such as:
- chanting (*Round and round the garden*)
- exploring different sound qualities and registers (*Round and round the garden*)
- vocalising to 'loo' or 'la' (*Mandy stands so big and tall*)
- singing nonsense words, humming (*Hey diddle diddle*)
- nasal sounds (*Christmas bells*)
- matching tone and dynamics (*Who made the pie?*)
- two parts: question and answer (*Who made the pie?*)
- singing at different tempi and dynamic levels (*To market, to market – lesson 8*)
- playing with words and consonants (*Little wind*)
- improvising (*My puppy* – lesson 33)
- pitch games (lesson 34)

Using the body

Physical action and movement are essential to musical performance and learning. Moving rhythmically to music helps young children to create a memory for musical patterns and structures, helping them to internalize.

Movement is pleasurable and expressive. Free movement, in response to a listening exercise, helps children to express the character and mood of music in a very visible and communicative way. It is a means of developing sensitivity in listening, performing and creating.

It may be used to develop a *rhythmic response* by promoting awareness of such things as steadiness of pulse, swinging or swaying 6/8 time, rhythm patterns, etc.

It is also helpful in fostering an *expressive response*, sensitizing children to the mood or character of a piece – is it light and airy? does it flow smoothly along?

Movement is also invaluable in encouraging a *creative response*, through imaginative individual and group movement improvisations and compositions.

Suggestions for movement range from actions of hands and feet in restricted space to paired activities and individual free movement. Year 1 children now are confident to perform simple actions or movement patterns. They progress to the freer use of space in which walking, jogging and striding to music become practised and controlled.

In this book suggestions for movement include:
- tapping and stepping the pulse (*Round and round the garden*)
- swinging or swaying (*Little wind*)
- tracing movements in the air (*Hey diddle diddle*)
- partner dances (*Two little birds*)
- playing a part in a singing game (*Mandy stands so big and tall*)
- moving freely in space (*Five currant buns*)
- relating different types of movement to tempo (*Just like me*)

Using instruments

Playing an instrument effectively is a most enjoyable experience. Technique and skills are required, however, to play even the simplest classroom instruments. Time is needed to 'play with', to explore, to practise and to refine.

At the infant stage, preparatory motor and co-ordination skills should be developed before putting an instrument into a child's hands. Many physical actions are suggested in this book (such as walking, or tapping a steady beat) as part of this necessary preparation.

With singing at the core, classroom instruments are gradually introduced as appropriate. Care should be taken to show children how to look after (expensive) instruments and to be aware of their own safety (particularly if pairs of cymbals are used).

Apart from instruments made in the classroom (see *Adventures in Music for the Very Young* by Gillian Wakely, Schott's *Beaters* series), children need access to a range of good quality instruments.

Untuned: hand drums, tambours, wood blocks, rhythm sticks or claves, triangles, cymbals, Indian bells or finger cymbals, tambourines, sleigh bells, maracas, guiros or scrapers, sandpaper blocks, cabasas

Tuned: chime bars: C D E F F♯ G A B♭ B C (ideally more than one set, and with lower bars G A B)
large bass bars (wooden): C, F and G
soprano and alto xylophones and glockenspiels

There is an increasing range of interesting African, Latin-American and Asian instruments which enriches instrumental resources immeasurably, e.g., African thumb piano (*mbira*), gato drum, cow-bells, small Indian harmonium.

A good supply of beaters or mallets is necessary (rubber heads for chime bars, felt or wool for xylophones, wooden or fibreglass for glockenspiels). Again, children need to be shown how to look after beaters, ensuring that beater heads are secure and not allowed to work or remain loose.

Peter Sidaway's *Strike Five* in Schott's *Beaters* series has excellent advice on all aspects of tuned percussion instruments and their use. Points to note are:

1. make sure that the longest (lowest) bars are on the left of the player;
2. if necessary, remove bars which are not needed (use both hands to grip them at each end);
3. bounce the beater on the middle of the bar so that it is allowed to vibrate.

Within this book instrumental work covers:

- exploring instrumental colour (*Hands are meant to clap*)
- matching a pattern (*Stars*)
- exploring sound effects (*Father and Mother and Uncle John*)
- playing a steady beat (*Five currant buns*)
- practising/creating music in the music corner (*Just like me, Little frog*)
- playing by ear (*The bear went over the mountain*)
- playing question and answer games (*Who made the pie?*)
- playing a drone (*Christmas bells*)
- performing to others (*Christmas bells*)
- distinguishing between instruments (*Jack Frost*)
- playing rhythm games (lesson 34)
- playing a solo part (*The band in the park*)

Teaching a song

There are several ways of teaching a song. Teachers may find that they need to be flexible in their approach, and adapt these suggestions to their own teaching context.

The most direct way is by 'patterning' or echoing back, where the teacher sings a line and the children imitate it (see *Round and round the garden*).

Another direct approach is to stage the process by breaking it down, first by chanting the rhythm (this occurs in *Mandy stands so big and tall*) or by getting the children to join in with the last few bars before singing to 'loo' or 'la'.

Very often, at this stage, the most natural or indirect way of teaching is to encourage children to join in – we say that the song is 'caught' rather than 'taught' (see *Five currant buns*).

Whichever way you choose, create a warm and confident atmosphere.

Accompanying songs

The majority are presented as a single melody line without accompaniment. Ideally the songs should stand alone, but chord symbols are provided should teachers wish to use a guitar or autoharp. There are piano accompaniments for some of the songs; some of these accompaniments incorporate the melody, but care must be taken not to drive the singing by playing the melody too loudly. An accompaniment exists to support and to enhance.

Organizing your lessons

Sessions will normally take place in the classroom – initially with the whole class, but also involving some group and individual work. This may be extended to other times of the day, with opportunities for continuing group and individual work within the classroom and in the music corner. Areas outside the classroom are often suitable for extending classwork, for example corridor space or the hall (particularly when locomotor movements are involved).

Single chime bars and hand-held percussion can be played standing or sitting, but glockenspiels and xylophones need to be played at a comfortable height on tables or on the floor with children kneeling in front of them. Whether in a group or as a class, much of the teaching will take place most effectively with children either sitting or standing in a three-quarter circle, maximizing eye contact.

Assessing and evaluating

You will wish to follow your own and your school's practice in recording achievement-levels. However, each lesson in this book ends with some suggested points of observation, and these can serve as a basis (or point of departure) for general or individual record-keeping.

It may be helpful, in addition to general evaluation of progress, to make a chart noting individual participation, accomplishment or any particular difficulties as they occur. In this way one builds a picture over a steady period. Such a chart, in producing a profile, will be useful for reporting to parents and recording the end-of-year picture for the receiving teacher.

1 Round and round the garden

Musical learning

Establishing musical experience through voice and body

Involvement in performing, active listening

Absorbing the musical elements of sound quality (timbre), pulse (steady beat), pitch (the melody) and voice register (high, low, medium)

Cross-curricular links

English: especially enunciation of consonants

Drama: role-play

General learning

Concentration (focused listening)

Imitation

Working as a class, and as an individual

Listening

Ask the class to listen as you chant and act out this familiar action song:

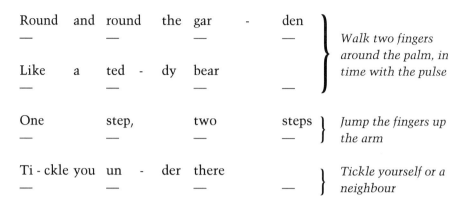

Use different vocal registers – high, low or medium pitch – and ask the children what kind of teddy bear they hear: young, grandfather, etc.

Performing

Find out which individual children can speak in different vocal registers for the rest of the class to identify. Take care not to strain anyone's voice. Introduce the notion of *tone quality* – a quavering voice, a gruff voice, etc.

Teach the song, unaccompanied, by singing one line at a time (patterning) for the children to imitate or echo back.

Tap out the pulse on the palm of your hand – two beats per bar. Can the children do this as they sing?

Assessment points

◆ How many children recognize the rhyme?

◆ Note their ability to recognize and imitate different registers.

◆ Who can tap the pulse while the song is sung?

2 Round and round the garden
Development lesson

Responding through invention, movement, mime, discussion

Sing through *Round and round the garden*.

Encourage suggestions for alternative animals in line 2, for example, 'like a little mouse', 'like a tall giraffe', 'like an elephant'.

Using a larger space, develop this activity into movement. Encourage the class to step around the room in time to the pulse as they sing.

Interpret the qualities of each animal by varying the tempo from slow (e.g. for an elephant) to fast (e.g. for a mouse).

At 'One step, two steps', etc. each child stops, takes two steps towards a partner, and they pretend to tickle each other.

As confidence develops, ask for volunteers to choose to be an animal. Ask the rest of the class to identify the animal after observing the kind of movement made. Discuss the contrasting qualities of movement: *heavy, weighty* for elephants; *light, fast* for birds; etc. This will help the children to acquire and practise new vocabulary.

Exploring sounds

Set out a range of different instruments, for instance:
- low chime or bass bars (for large, heavy animals)
- high bars or soprano glockenspiels (for small, light creatures)
- scrapers or guiros (for insects)

Discuss which would be appropriate for different kinds of animals. Invite individual children in turn to explore the sounds that they can produce from different instruments.

Listening and responding

Play short extracts from 'The elephant' and 'The aviary' from *Carnival of the Animals* by Saint-Saëns. Ask the children to listen first; then play the extracts again, and ask them to move in the way that their imagined animal moves.

Assessment points

◆ Which children are keen to make alternative animal suggestions?

◆ How well do children choose instruments to represent particular animals or creatures?

◆ What do they notice about the sounds made?

Musical learning

Sense of pulse

Experience of tempo: fast and slow

Sound exploration: pitch and timbre of different instruments

Expressive use of these musical elements

Listening: Saint-Saëns' Carnival of the Animals

Cross-curricular links

Drama: mime

Nature: the different ways animals move

General learning

Imagination, ideas

Social skills: working with a partner

Observing, interpreting

3 Hey diddle diddle

Musical learning

Tempo: slow/fast

Pitch: up and down, melodic contour

Pulse: swaying rhythm

Movement to music (responding to pitch and pulse)

Listening: a swaying piece (Fauré's Berceuse *or Chopin's* Barcarolle)

Remind the children of *Hickory, dickory, dock* (*Targeting Music* Reception Year, p. 10).

Here is another rhyme with similar characteristics:

Hey diddle, diddle, the cat and the fiddle,
The cow jumped over the moon.
The little dog laughed to see such fun
And the dish ran away with the spoon.

Sing *Hey diddle diddle* at a modest pace.

Sing and recite it, practising it over and over again, adopting different speeds (tempi) until the children have 'caught' the song. Discuss the humour of the idea.

Responding with graphic movement

Show with your arms how the music flows up and down, emphasizing the stepward rising movement at 'see such fun and the dish'.

Now sing it to these nonsense words:

> Did-dle-dy did-dle-dy did-dle-dy did-dle-dy
> Dum-dy did-dle-dy dummm
> Oh, did-dle-dy dum-dy dum-dy did-dle-dy
> Did-dle-dy did-dle-dy dummm.

(Make sure that 'dummm' really hums, producing a sensation in the nose.)

Mark the pulse, by swinging or swaying.

Help the children to notice how the tune 'climbs the stairs' at 'see such fun'. Mark this rise by demonstrating how we can rise up to a standing position at the climax of this phrase ('the dish').

Ask the children to listen carefully, and recognize when the music tells them to rise, and when to sink down to a sitting position.

Encourage the children to sway to the pulse:
- by themselves
- with a partner, holding one hand
- facing a partner, holding both hands and swaying back and forth
- facing a partner, swaying side to side

Listening and responding

Play the children another swaying piece, for instance:
- Fauré: 'Berceuse' from *Dolly Suite*
- Chopin: *Barcarolle*

Cross-curricular links

Language: enunciation of consonants

General learning

Imagination: humour

Social skills: working with a partner

Assessment points

◆ How well do the children articulate the words?

◆ Who can sing any part of the song by him- or herself?

◆ How many children can sway in time to the song? (The majority, some, a few?)

◆ Do the children work well with a partner?

4 *Hey diddle diddle*
Development lesson

Check how well everyone can remember *Hey diddle diddle.*

Ask if anyone knows what a fiddle is. Does anyone know another name for a fiddle? Do cats normally play fiddles?

Singing and moving (miming)

Ask the children to pretend that they have fiddles, holding them up to their shoulders and necks, with bows ready. Instead of swaying to the pulse, ask them to pretend to bow their imaginary violin. Prepare them to get ready for the strong down bow.

Demonstrate how to sing the song while bowing steady ♩. beats down and up from the beginning to the halfway point.

How many bows are there? (eight). Try bowing for half the song and resting for the other half.

Moving in space

Ask the children to put down their imaginary bows and get ready to find the running patterns in the music (the quavers, especially the running quavers at the beginning and end of the tune).

Now ask one group to sing while another runs or jogs, very lightly. (If space is restricted, instead of running or jogging use fingers to tap on arms.) Change over.

Get one group to sing while another bows. The singing should match the strength and energy of the movement. (Bowing should create loud, heavy, energetic tone. Jogging or tapping should create soft, light tone.)

Emphasize the link between loud or soft tone, and the movements which engendered these qualities.

More movements may be tried out in open space – for instance, *walking* the steady beat instead of bowing it. Alternate this with light running or jogging of the quavers.

Musical learning

Manner of playing a violin

Pulse, contrasted with rhythm patterns

Expression: light or heavy tone

Optional piano accompaniment

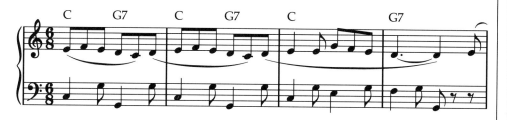

Assessment points

◆ How well was the song remembered?

◆ Which children were familiar with fiddles or violins?

◆ How well could children mark the beat?

◆ At what speed could children master the running pattern?

5 Little wind

Words: Kate Greenaway
Music: DT

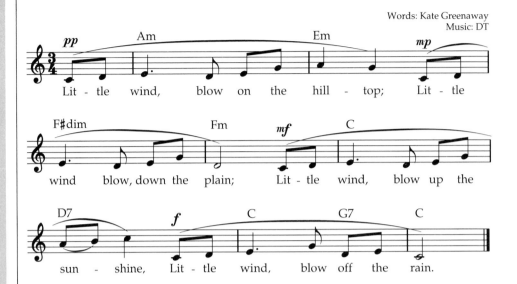

Little wind, blow on the hilltop;
Little wind, blow down the plain;
Little wind, blow up the sunshine,
Little wind, blow off the rain.

Musical learning

Vocal technique: phrasing, breath control

Pitch: melodic contour

Swaying 3/4 rhythm

Expression in performance: different dynamic levels; crescendo; making an introduction

Listening and singing

Teach this song line by line. Present a good model by sustaining one breath right through each phrase, using arms and hands at the ends of each line to trace the rise and fall of the melody.

Singing and moving

Encourage a swaying movement to this song. With a partner, children might sway from side to side, in this way helping to put energy into the stressed notes (wind, hill, wind, plain, etc.).

Performing

Start the song really softly and build up to a loud finish.

Then divide the class into two halves and try singing it line by line in turn. Some children might care to sing by themselves.

Suggest to the children that they make a little introduction by saying softly over and over again:

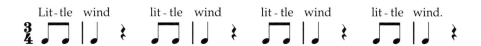

Assessment points

◆ Are most of the children able to sing with clear diction?

◆ Are most able to sing in tune, at least within a range of six notes?

◆ How rhythmically – but softly – can the class chant the 'little wind' introduction?

Cross-curricular links

Language: vocabulary

General learning

Working together for a purpose

17

6 Little wind
Development lesson

Musical learning

Exploring and describing sounds

Choosing and controlling sounds – tone colour and dynamics

Inventing and performing

Listening: Mussorgsky's Night on the Bare Mountain

Listening and Imagining

Ask the children to imagine leaves lying thickly on the ground – perhaps in a wood or park. Discuss their colour, their feel, the sound they make when you walk through them.

Read the poem:

Beech leaves

> In autumn down the beechwood path
> The leaves lie thick upon the ground.
> It's there I love to kick my way
> And hear the crisp and crashing sound.
>
> *James Reeves*

Exploring word sounds

Focus on the words 'crisp' and 'crashing', asking the class to say them over and over again. Start to add more words beginning with a 'c', like 'crinkly', 'crunching', 'crackling'. Play with the sheer colour of these sounds.

Exploring instrumental sounds

Lay out a selection of instruments, such as:
- maracas, sleigh bells, tambourines – for shaking
- guiros, sandpaper blocks – for scraping
- drums, tambours, Indian bells, triangles – for beating or striking

Encourage exploration and experimentation. Enable four children at a time to choose an instrument each, and explore the different sound sources. As they do this, engage the rest of the class in describing the kinds of sounds they hear.

Choosing sounds, inventing, performing

Choose appropriate sounds to play after the last line of the poem. How should the sounds be played: loudly, softly, starting soft and making a crescendo, slowly, fast? End with a class performance.

Listening and imagining

In contrast, listen to an extract from Mussorgsky's *Night on the Bare Mountain* to hear a more powerful depiction of strong winds and storm.

Assessment points

◆ Which children need encouragement with language?

◆ Does ability with language necessarily correspond with observable musical development?

◆ How controlled were children in playing softly, making a crescendo?

7 Father and Mother and Uncle John

Playing an individual part at the right time

'Cantering' rhythm pattern:

Playing a controlled crescendo (getting louder)

Rhythmic movement

Music: DT

Fa-ther and Mo-ther and Un-cle John   Went to mar-ket one   by one.

Fa-ther fell off.   (!)   Mo-ther fell off.   (!)   But

Un-cle John went on   and on   and   on   and on   and on.

Father and Mother and Uncle John
Went to market one by one.
Father fell off.
Mother fell off.
But Uncle John went on and on and on and on and on.

Listening and performing

Teach this rhyme by first singing it through slowly, patting the steady beat on your legs. Mark the last, long note by bringing arms up and round to form a circle, to show how the sound is sustained.

Now chant the words in rhythm.

Once the song is becoming known, lengthen the silences or rests where Father falls off and Mother falls off. Introduce a vocal or instrumental sound effect – e.g. swanee whistle, scraper, vibraslap – to mark this feature. Or mark it with a sudden silence!

While having this joke, discuss what is happening. How far do they fall? What have they fallen off? Ask if any child would like to play an instrument to create the sound effect.

Stand up and sing the song again.

Introduce a drum or tambour to mark the ♩ ♪♩ ♪ rhythm, representing the sound of cantering horses or ponies.

Can we play the drum as if the horses were gradually getting nearer? (Introduce the terms 'soft', 'louder'.) *How* can we play to make the music get louder? (With two fingers, then three, then four, then the whole hand.)

Show another way of getting louder (gradually using more energy).

Singing, moving, enacting

In a larger space make a big circle. Choose one child to be Mother, one to be Father and another to be Uncle John.

The rest of the class hold hands and, while singing, mark the steady beat by moving their arms up and down in time. Father, Mother and Uncle John canter round the inside of the circle pretending to fall off, or going on and on as appropriate.

After several turns to ensure the participation of all who wish to take these parts, divide the class into two. Ask half the class to be Uncle John cantering around while the other half stands still and sings the song. (Make a rule: while cantering, not to touch another person.)

Change the groups over.

An optional piano accompaniment is provided on page 80. Alternatively, you may prefer to play just the melody line with hands one octave apart.

Cross-curricular links

Drama: mime; enacting a role

General learning

Taking an individual part

Assessment points

◆ How quickly are the words learned?

◆ How well have individual children learned the tune?

◆ Are children singing and moving at the same time?

◆ Which children tend to lead, which tend to follow?

8 Father and Mother and Uncle John

Development lesson

Musical learning

'Cantering' rhythm

Tempo: fast, slow, getting faster

Dynamics: crescendo

Expression: varied when singing, between soft/light and loud/heavy

Chanting and singing

Sing *Father and Mother and Uncle John* again. Then introduce another chant with a cantering rhythm:

> To market, to market to buy a fat pig,
> Home again, home again, jiggety jig.

Teach the song by singing and playing it at a steady tempo. (There is a piano accompaniment on page 82.)

To market, to market to buy a fat pig

Music: DT

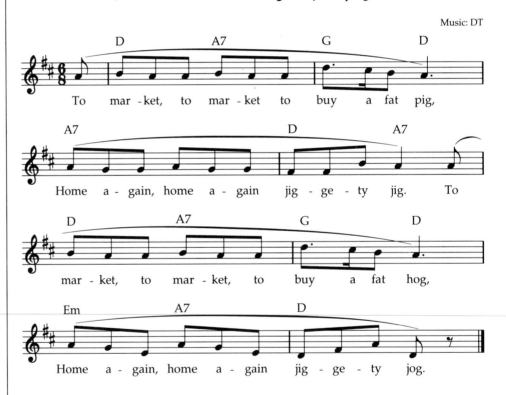

Try it at a faster tempo, and then a slower one.

Next, introduce *This is the way the ladies ride* (see opposite). This is a much longer song, best picked up over a period of time. It starts softly and lightly, but then gets gradually louder and heavier.

There is a piano accompaniment on pages 80–81.

This is the way the ladies ride

This is the way the ladies ride,
    Nim, nim, nim, nim.
This is the way the gentlemen ride,
    Trim, trim, trim, trim.
This is the way the farmers ride,
    Trot, trot, trot, trot.
This is the way the huntsmen ride,
    A-gallop, a-gallop, a-gallop, a-gallop.
This is the way the plough boys ride,
    Hobbledy-gee, hobbledy-gee, hobbledy-gee.
(spoken) And down into a DITCH!

Assessment points

◆ Are most children able to adjust to the different tempi?

◆ Which individuals grasp the concept of getting gradually louder?

Cross-curricular links

Language: vocabulary, enunciation

English: heritage of traditional rhymes

General learning

Performance: participation in controlled collective changes of speed and expression

9 Two little birds

Music: DT

Two lit - tle birds   Sit - ting on   a hill,

One named Jack,   One named Jill.

Fly   a - way__ Jack,   Fly   a - way__ Jill,

Come back Jack,   Come back   Jill.

Two little birds
Sitting on a hill,
One named Jack,
One named Jill.
Fly away Jack,
Fly away Jill,
Come back Jack,
Come back Jill.

This finger rhyme, manipulating hands and forefingers, requires greater dexterity than action songs. You may care to make finger puppets out of felt or card and decorate them simply, to represent Jack and Jill, before presenting the song.

Listening

Sing and enact the song. There are many ways in which the finger actions can be done. Whichever way you choose, endeavour to make your movements rhythmical, showing the steady beat throughout the song.

Listening and moving

Next, ask the children to imitate your actions. There is no need to teach the song line by line – children are absorbing:
1) the idea, the fun and enjoyment
2) the steady pulse (from the steady rhythmic way in which you sing and perform it)
3) sound and silence (making the rests significant)

Singing

Encourage the children to sing when they can, repeating it many times over. Choose a very steady speed or tempo and stick to it.

Make sure that you do not sing through the rests.

Assessment points

◆ How quickly do the children learn to sing this song?

◆ Do most children grasp the idea of 'rests' in music?

◆ Can your class sing and perform, keeping a steady tempo?

Musical learning

Pitch: melodic contour, relationship of two notes (higher/lower)

Invention: choosing instrumental sounds

♩ ♩ ♩ 𝄽

rhythm pattern

10 *Two little birds*
Development lesson

Listening and responding

Before you revise the song, ask the children to imagine the birds.

Can they also help you to show the shape of the melody – sometimes up, sometimes down – as you sing?

Ask: Is it a high hill? Did the birds fly up to the hill? Show the movement with your hands.

Assist musical understanding by showing the melodic contour, facing the children, using both hands. You can show high and low pitches, movement up and down, and also length of notes, in this way.

Which notes are higher than others? For example:

One

      named   Jack

Performing

Children may wish to take turns in playing the parts of the two birds, flying away and coming back again to the centre of a circle made by the rest of the class.

Instrumental extension

Add an instrumental effect for the flying away and another for coming back again. Ask the children to choose from a range of tuned instruments laid out for this purpose. Which has the appropriate tone colour? Swanee whistle? A glissando on a glockenspiel, or on a xylophone?

Movement extension

The children choose a partner and face each other.

Sing the song. Everyone claps their partner's hands to this pattern:

    1, 2, 3, break

until the very last bar, where the end of the song is marked by patting the same pattern on the thighs.

Ask for suggestions for a silent gesture in the rest.

To mark 'Fly away Jack, fly away Jill', introduce the idea of taking backward steps:

    step, step, step, (stop)

and then forward steps for the 'Come back' phrases:

    step, step, step, (stop)

This

    1   2   3   rest
    ♩ ♩ ♩ 𝄽   pattern can also be done by the children in a
  step step step (stop)

long file.

Assessment points

◆ Is there a ready response to playing an instrumental sound?

◆ Can individuals co-ordinate their rhythmic actions?

11 Incy Wincy Spider

Musical learning

Feeling for steady 6/8 pulse

Another finger rhyme. In this version the melody line follows the up and down movement of the poem.

Music: DT

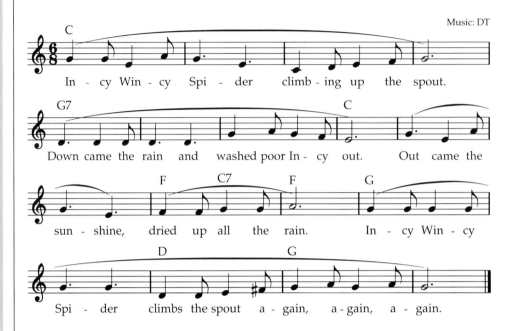

In - cy Win - cy Spi - der climb - ing up the spout. Down came the rain and washed poor In - cy out. Out came the sun - shine, dried up all the rain. In - cy Win - cy Spi - der climbs the spout a - gain, a - gain, a - gain.

Incy Wincy Spider climbing up the spout,
Down came the rain and washed poor Incy out.
Out came the sunshine, dried up all the rain.
Incy Wincy spider climbs the spout again, again, again.

28

Listening and singing

First speak the lines according to the rhythm, showing the actions as you do so.

Then sing the first two bars, and ask the children to echo them back to you.

Do this three or four times until well established.

Teach the song using this echoing-back approach, phrase by phrase, until all four lines are memorized.

Do not labour the teaching, should attention flag. Work on the basis of short, concentrated bursts.

Music corner activity

In the music corner, make a spout (from card) and a spider (from pipe cleaners, perhaps?).

Write out and mount the words of the song so that children can visit the corner individually and recall as much as they can of the song.

Cross-curricular links

Language: reading the words of the song

General learning

Showing initiative: working as an individual

Assessment points

◆ Note how many children pick up the idea of 'echoing'.

◆ How quickly is the song learned?

◆ Which children go to the music corner, and how many can be heard singing the song?

12 Incy Wincy Spider
Development lesson

Performing

Sing the song again.

Encourage the children to stand and do Incy's actions. Use whole-body movement in pretending to climb the spout again.

Singing, learning about the voice

Ask what their voice does when singing 'climbing up the spout'.

Help the children to physically feel their voice as the vibrations travel up from the throat into the head cavity (place hand on throat, then cup face and chin, then fingers on the sides of the forehead).

Sing it to 'doo' – this produces a stronger vibration in the lower areas.

Then try experimenting with high notes and low notes, to feel different strengths and locations of vibrations.

Singing game

Make a circle with the children.

One child stands in the middle and acts out the story while the rest of the class walk round in time to the steady ♩. beat.

Everyone stops on 'again', and keeps still for two bars.

Exploring and improvising

Set out a selection of six or seven tuned and untuned instruments, and encourage the children to make up some music to suggest the *spider*, the *rain* and the *sunshine.*

Afterwards these instruments could be placed in the music corner. Make an attractive display or work-card which invites children – first by themselves and later in pairs – to:
- 'Make up some music which tells us it's raining – a rain piece'.
- 'Compose some music which tells us it's a sunny day.'

Provide opportunities for them to perform to the class and talk about their music. 'Why did you choose these instruments?' 'How did you start?'

Cross-curricular links

Drama: mime

Science: vibrations, voice-production

General learning

Self-expression and discussion

Assessment points

◆ Which children enjoy locating their voice?

◆ Which children are keen to play instruments?

◆ What kind of differences appear in the music they make? (length, design, ideas, imagination, sense of rhythm, feeling for pitch)

13 Christmas bells

Christ-mas bells are ring-ing, Chil-dren's voi-ces sing-ing.

What do they say? What do they say?

Lit - tle Je - su's born to - day.

Refrain

Ding dong, ding dong,

Ding ding dong.

1. Christmas bells are ringing,
   Children's voices singing.
   What do they say?
   What do they say?
   Little Jesu's born today.

   > Ding dong, ding dong,
   > Ding ding dong.

2. Christmas trees are all alight
   With lovely colours.
   What do they say?
   What do they say?
   Little Jesu's born today.

   > Ding dong, *etc.*

Listening and performing

Teach this song by patterning, singing the verse to the syllable 'la'. Encourage the children to feel the swinging 3/4 pulse by holding hands and swaying from side to side.

Enjoy the nasal sensation of singing long notes on 'ding' and 'dong', by moving quickly to the 'ng' sound rather than holding on to the vowel.

Make an echo effect of the first four phrases, singing the first moderately loudly and the second softly, the third moderately loudly and the fourth softly.

On the long-held action words of the refrain, show the children how to pull the bells with long energetic swings.

Perform the song with the children pulling imaginary bells all the way through.

If desired, make up extra verses with the help of the children.

Listening and responding

Play 'Carillons' from Bizet's *L'Arlésienne*, prompting the children to pull imaginary bells when they recognize the bell-like sounds.

Cross-curricular links

Drama: mime

Physical Education: energetic movements

Language: enunciation; inventing extra verses

General learning

Co-operation in performance

Assessment points

◆ Are most of the children able to articulate the words of the first two lines at a modest speed?

◆ Can they sing the refrain with energy?

◆ Are they able to pull the imaginary bell rope with energy, and time it rhythmically?

◆ How many children can control their singing, alternating between loud and soft?

Musical learning

Learning: about drones

Singing in 2 parts, playing in 2 parts

14 Christmas bells
Development lesson

Optional piano accompaniment

Instrumental extension

Take a middle C chime bar and play it on the first beat of each bar, as children sing and pull on the bells. Tell them that this is a **drone**.

Give individual children turns to play the chime bar, while the rest of the class sing and pull their imaginary bells.

Now set out three G chime bars on one side and three C chime bars on the other. Invite *all* the class to imagine that they are playing these during the refrain, with the children sitting on the G side playing the Gs and the children sitting on the C side playing the Cs. Now *sing* the refrain only, with the G children singing only the Gs and the C children singing only the Cs. Teacher conducts, helping the two groups to come in at the right time.

Invite six children at a time to play the instruments. Everyone helps by singing their respective notes.

Share a class performance with another group of children.

Music corner extension

In the music corner, set out C and G chime bars for children to practise on.

Follow this up with metallophones or sets of chime bars which children can use to make up their own bell tune.

Assessment points

◆ How many children can time their playing to coincide with the strong beat?

◆ Which children are developing technical control of the beater?

15 Jack Frost

Musical learning

Expressive use of articulation: staccato and legato styles of singing

Percussion instruments: playing techniques

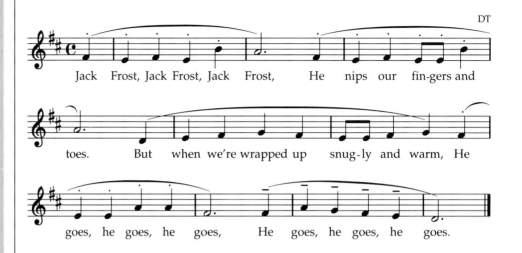

Jack Frost, Jack Frost, Jack Frost, He nips our fin-gers and toes. But when we're wrapped up snug-ly and warm, He goes, he goes, he goes, He goes, he goes, he goes.

Jack Frost, Jack Frost, Jack Frost,
He nips our fingers and toes.
But when we're wrapped up snugly and warm,
He goes, he goes, he goes,
He goes, he goes, he goes.

Listening and performing

In teaching this song, point up the sharpness and angularity of the first, second and fourth phrases. Detach the sounds as marked (staccato). In contrast 'But when we're wrapped up...' is smooth (legato). The final phrase 'He goes, he goes, he goes' should be more weighty, each sound receiving emphasis.

Actions will help children to anticipate the words.

Singing game

Once learned, this song can be performed as a singing game.

Make a circle and, with joined hands, move round in an anti-clockwise direction.

> line 1: tiptoe until end of line when you 'freeze' on the spot.
> line 2: the same.
> line 3: move into the centre in a big 'huggle'.
> line 4: stay there.
> line 5: move back into original starting position ready to begin again.

Alternatively, if there is sufficient space, your class can move independently as individuals.

> line 1: tiptoe until end of line when you 'freeze' on the spot.
> line 2: the same.
> line 3: remain in place, wrap both arms around yourself.
> line 4: tiptoe and freeze.
> line 5: stamp and freeze.

Instrumental extension

Select a guiro or wood block, and a tambourine, and show how two people can accompany the first phrase using a shaken tambourine for the long note and the guiro or wood block for the staccato notes.

How would the children like to accompany the rest of the song?

Assessment points

◆ Can the children sing detached sounds and sustained sounds?

◆ In the singing game, are their movements controlled?

◆ How well can individual children control their instrumental sounds?

Cross-curricular links

Dance: control of tip-toeing, freezing, stamping

Drama: mime

Geography: seasons

General learning

Control and co-ordination in a large group

16 Jack Frost
Development lesson

Musical learning

Exploring word sounds

Inventing and expressing: choosing and organizing instrumental sounds

Notating: 'drawing' their music on paper

Listening: Vivaldi's Four Seasons, *Debussy's* Children's Corner Suite

Word-sound exploration

Suggest that there are other weather rhymes by first whispering these two lines from a well-known rhyme:

> Watch out, watch out, Jack Frost is about,
> He's after our fingers and toes.

Talk about winter and the words that are associated with it.

Then present another weather rhyme:

> Spring is showery, flowery, bowery,
> Summer: hoppy, croppy, poppy,
> Autumn: slippy, drippy, nippy,
> Winter: breezy, sneezy, freezy.

Teach the poem, and then play with the words to point up the sharp contrasts between the seasons – particularly between winter and summer.

Inventing with instruments

Help the children to select instruments and sounds from which to create 'icy', 'sharp' and 'snowy' weather pictures in sound.

Notating

Record the children's ideas on tape. Can the children 'draw' their music in some way on paper, so that they can remember what they have played?

Be open to the varied ways in which young children choose to 'represent' music.

Listening and responding

Introduce the children to some music with a similar theme. Two possibilities would be 'Winter' from Vivaldi's *Four Seasons,* and 'Snow is dancing' from Debussy's *Children's Corner Suite.*

Encourage the class to close their eyes and listen. On the second hearing of the Debussy, ask them to move their hands and arms in time with the music to show the snow falling – fast and light.

Engage the children in the music by encouraging them to respond to it in different ways. Ask them to move around the hall or room. Or, on another occasion, ask them to draw what they hear, or to talk about the music, telling everyone how the music sounds.

Cross-curricular links

Language: poetry, onomatopoeia, vocabulary, discussion

Drama: expressive gesture

Art: drawing/painting

General learning

Expressing, relating and responding in different ways

Assessment points

◆ Notice which children are able to talk easily about music and sound.

◆ Note the different ways in which children record their ideas on paper.

◆ Note the ways in which children respond to the listening task.

17 Five currant buns in a baker's shop

1. Five currant buns in a baker's shop,
   Round and fat with sugar on the top.
   Along came a boy with a penny one day,
   Bought a currant bun and took it away.

2. Four currant buns ...
       etc.

Listening and performing

Discuss the baker's shop, or the bakery section in the local supermarket. Think about favourite cakes and buns – iced cakes, doughnuts, etc. Adapt the words of the song to the children's favourite foods.

Play the game with children representing currant buns or other cakes.

The song is learned as the game is played.

The rhythm of the words is almost more important than the pitch.

When the song and the game are well known, start introducing these variations:

Variation 1
All the class does the actions. Teacher sings, and the children join in singing in their own time. At the third phrase choose an individual to sing: 'Along came a boy (or girl) with a penny one day'. Then everyone joins in again for the fourth phrase.

Variation 2
(This aims to foster an inner picture of the music – an aural image.)
> Sing the song until the last line, which is mimed.
> Then sing lines 1 and 2 and mime 3 and 4.
> Then sing 1 and mime the rest.
> Finally, mime it all.

Have a signal for 'mime' – finger up in the air – and for 'sound' – an upward or outwardly stretched hand. Make signs for children to hold saying 'currant bun 1p'.

Cross-curricular links

Language: discussion

Drama: mime, acting out

Mathematics: counting down

General learning

Co-operating: taking a turn, working in a group

Assessment points

◆ How soon do the children fit actions to words?

◆ How deftly do they co-ordinate their miming actions?

◆ Ask on another occasion who can remember enough of this song to sing the beginning, or can remember all of it?

18 Five currant buns in a baker's shop
Development lesson

Performing and responding

Revise the song.

Next, seat the children in a circle. Ask everyone to sing the song while miming a walking action with their arms and hands.

Once this can be done ask everyone to stand up and walk around the room, using as much space as possible, singing the song and walking in time to the steady beat (2 beats per bar).

Ask one child to keep time with rhythm sticks, wood block or tambourine, while the others sing and walk. Introduce a second instrument, with a contrasting sound, then a third, a fourth and a fifth.

Let each child play in turn. Ask children to pass their instrument around so that, in time, everyone has a turn on a variety of instruments.

The aim is to build up the experience of keeping a steady beat in as many different ways as possible – walking hands, walking bodies, and playing instruments.

Optional piano accompaniment

Assessment points

◆ Do the children sing well together?

◆ Is everyone keen to take a turn with an instrument?

◆ How many children can mark a steady beat continuously with
  hands?
  marching?
  on an instrument?

19 I'm a little teapot

Musical learning

Pulse

Dynamics

Accented notes

Long notes and short notes

I'm a little teapot, short and stout.
Here's my handle, here's my spout!
When I get my steam up, hear me shout,
Tip me up, and pour me out.

Listening and performing

Encourage the children to tap the pulse quietly with you as you sing the song – until the last line, when they can clap the pulse loudly.

Think of different ways to mark the pulse. Invite suggestions, e.g. tapping shoulders, tapping own head, tapping feet, shrugging shoulders. Still maintain a fairly quiet performance until the last line.

Teach the words and melody, line by line if necessary, and finally mime the actions suggested by the words.

Singing inevitably suffers when children are asked to do too many things at the same time, so ask the children now to alternate with you. First, teacher does the actions, children sing the song. Then change over.

Next, introduce the marking of the pulse, by tapping or clapping, while singing. Give a loud tap or clap on 'Tip', to show the strong accent on that note. Discuss the effect of this accent with your children.

Investigating

Ask which words have the longest sounds in this song? 'Spout', 'shout', 'tip'...?

Practise some long sounds. Who can sing a long sound, choosing their own comfortable note?

Which words have the shortest sounds in this song?

Who can sing a short sound – a very short sound?

Cross-curricular links

Language: vocabulary, enunciation

Drama: mime

General learning

Sorting

Assessment points

◆ Were the actions correct?

◆ Could the words be heard?

◆ Are the children able to mark the pulse accurately while singing?

Musical learning

*Pitch: concept of
high/low,
higher/lower; melodic
contour*

*'Notation': graphic
representation of
pitch*

20 *I'm a little teapot*
(*Development lesson*)

Sing *I'm a little teapot,* noting how many children remember it easily.

Singing and conceptualizing

Draw this rough outline of the first two bars on the blackboard or flip chart:

I'm   a   lit-tle   tea- pot short and   stout

With your back half-turned to the children trace the shape with your hand and invite the children to do the same in the air.

Now draw the shape of the last two bars:

Tip   me up and pour me out

Ask if anyone has noticed anything about these shapes. (The first goes up and the second goes down.)

Make sure that you always sing the shape as the children trace it in the air.

'High' or 'low', 'going up' or 'going down' – the up-and-down concept of pitch is artificial, so it is helpful to reinforce melodic contour in as many concrete ways as possible.

Ask individual children to come out and, as everyone sings, trace along the shape with their index finger.

As an extension to this children can draw their own shapes on pieces of paper using any of their mathematical equipment (counters, rods, etc.) to represent what you have shown to the whole class.

Make connections to other songs where there are similar rises and falls, for example the last line of *Hey diddle diddle* or the first and last lines of *Hickory, dickory, dock.*

Assessment points

◆ How many children can talk about this experience?

◆ Do most individuals find it easy to trace in the air as everyone sings?

◆ How many can extend this classwork by drawing and identifying musical shapes? How well do they do this?

21 Hands are meant to clap

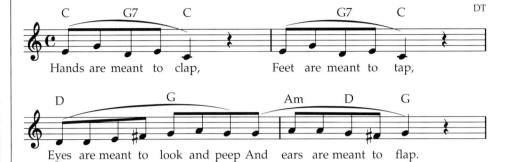

Hands are meant to clap,   Feet are meant to tap,

Eyes are meant to look and peep And ears are meant to flap.

Knees are meant to bend,   Arms are meant to move,

Legs are meant to jump up high And heads to reach the roof!

Hands are meant to clap,
Feet are meant to tap,
Eyes are meant to look and peep
And ears are meant to flap.

Knees are meant to bend,
Arms are meant to move,
Legs are meant to jump up high
And heads to reach the roof!

Listening and performing

Make a large circle with freedom to move on the spot.

Bar 1: over the four beats, clap hands 1, 2, 3, and on the fourth beat push your hands outwards as if invisibly clapping the hands of a partner.

Bar 2: tap your feet alternately, 1, 2, 3, and on the fourth beat kick your free leg in the air.

Practise these two phrases with everyone doing the actions.

Carry out a similar sequence for the eyes and the ears.

Repeat from the beginning, at least twice.

Teach the second half of the song in the same way. Make sure that it is all sung steadily, at an even tempo. Children will enjoy turning to face a partner while singing the song.

Listening and investigating

Discuss the silent gaps when nothing happens. Say 'How quiet can we make those silent beats?'

And 'Show me when the music goes up.'

Instrumental extension

While the class is singing the song, could an individual child clap a

♩ ♩ ♩ ♪ repeated pattern (ostinato) throughout?

When fluent, the pattern could be transferred to a tambour or wood block.

Assessment points

◆ Are the children able to sing and do the actions:
   a) with you?
   b) with your action-prompts, but without vocal prompting?
   c) rhythmically, with co-ordinated voice and actions?

Musical learning

Expression/compos-
ing: exploring,
choosing and
organizing sounds

Rhythmic playing

22 *Hands are meant to clap*
Development lesson

Instrumental extension

Ask the children to think of animals they like.

Encourage them to make up a poem with a similar rhythm pattern to *Hands are meant to clap*. For example:

> Worms are good at wriggling,
> Birds are good at pecking, ...

Choose an instrument to illustrate the notion of wriggling (e.g. swanee whistle), and another to illustrate pecking birds (e.g. guiro).

What other animals? What other actions?

Performing, improvising and composing

Explore instrumental sounds with the children, encouraging them to think about the tone qualities of different instruments, and how they might be matched to the qualities of the animals and birds.

Here are some possible ways of using the sounds:

1. Play the instrument with the rhythm of the words.
2. Play the instrument at the end of the line, in the silent space before the next line.
3. Make up a sound-picture to depict the various animals and birds in your poem.

Place pictures or photographs of different animals in the music corner, and encourage small groups to make their own animal sounds.

Or you could organize children into groups of four or five to extend what you have been doing as a class. Ask them to work on creating a piece of music without any words, on the subject of 'The Animal World'.

They will need to consider:
- which animal ideas they wish to use
- how to start
- who will start
- who will stop
- when to stop

Assessment points

◆ How many children can control an instrument:
   a) rhythmically, with the words?
   b) in the silent space?

◆ Which children are good at organizing themselves as groups?

23 Mandy stands so big and tall

DT

Man-dy stands so big and tall, Stretch-es far a - bove us all.

She can dance, she can sing, She can do most a - ny - thing._____

Musical learning

Pulse

Cross-curricular links

Dance: singing game with actions

General learning

Taking solo and group roles

Mandy stands so big and tall,
Stretches far above us all.
She can dance, she can sing,
She can do most anything.

Listening and performing

Using a name unfamiliar to the class, teach the song first by chanting it to the given rhythm.

Next sing it to the melody, repeating it until it has been grasped.

Grouping the children in a circle, ask for a volunteer to do the actions – either in the centre of the circle or standing in place.

The soloist performs the actions suggested and, when ready, introduces any action he or she likes. The music stops, everyone imitates (for example, a hopping or jumping action) for an appropriate length of time before another soloist is chosen and the song is restarted.

Finally, why not sing a verse where 'everybody' is substituted for the name (or use the name of the class).

Next, while singing the song, tap the beat in different ways – for example, tapping one's legs or shoulders.

Arrange turns to play the steady beat on untuned percussion: one instrument to the circle (e.g. tambourine, wood block, rhythm sticks, sleigh bells). While one child has a turn, the rest join in clapping.

Explain that this is the steady beat, or pulse.

Assessment points

◆ How confidently do the children volunteer to be soloists?

◆ Can children time their actions?

◆ Can most of the children tap a steady beat?

24 Mandy stands so big and tall
Development lesson

Revision

Start off by miming the actions of the song – can the children recall it? Help them to remember the words and melody. Get them to *sing* a line and *think* a line.

Go over some of the previous lesson. Can the children remember *what* it was they were performing when tapping, clapping or playing percussion?

Performing a rhythm pattern

Next, focus everyone's attention on the ♫ ♩ rhythm pattern.

Start by picking out the isolated phrases: 'big and tall', ''bove us all', 'she can dance' and 'she can sing'. Clap them, and say them to the French time names 'ta-te-taa': ♫ ♩

ta - te - taa

(The French time-names, like sol-fa syllables, remain constant in defining rhythm values.)

Carry on with this rhythm, asking the children to join you, encouraging all the class, and individuals who wish to try by themselves.

In pairs, facing a partner, ask the children to clap each other's hands while saying the rhythm 'ta-te-taa'.

Sing the song and clap hands whenever the ♫ ♩ rhythm arrives.

Instrumental extension

Hand out pairs of untuned instruments and encourage two children at a time to play the ♫ ♩ pattern while the rest of the class sing.

Then divide the class into two halves to practise this pattern, one half echoing or imitating the other.

At other times, present the opportunity for children to make up their own rhythm patterns.

Assessment points

◆ Can the children internalize, or inwardly 'think', the music?

◆ How soon do they perform the rhythm pattern as individuals, or with a partner?

◆ Who can perform it on an instrument?

Musical learning

'Internalizing' music

Pulse

♫ ♩
('ta - te - taa')
rhythm pattern

General learning

Internalizing: awareness of how to 'think' a previously heard process

25 Just like me

Will you walk around the room just like me?
Will you walk around the room just like me, me, me?
Will you walk around the room just like a busy, busy bee?
Will you walk around the room just like me, me, me?

Listening and performing

Teach this song by doing it, with the children joining in. Make it rhythmic, with a firm, steady beat. Encourage the children to use all the space available and find different directions to walk in.

Positive use of space is helped by adding the following verses:

2. Will you hop across the floor *(slower speed)*
   ... just like a busy, busy flea?

3. Will you creep along the wall *(twice as slow as the walk)*
   ... then you can see what you can see?

4. Will you sway from side to side *(slow, steady beat)*
   ... will you be a swaying tree?

5. Will you jog on the spot *(twice as fast as the walk)*
   ... getting very, very hot!

Ask the children to suggest other verses.

Listening and responding

Other songs may be employed to reinforce the relationship between tempo and type of movement:

- walking: *The grand old Duke of York* (p. 83), *If all the world were paper* (p. 88)
- jaunty walking: *London Bridge is broken down* (p. 85)
- hopping: *Aiken Drum* (p. 86), *Pop goes the weasel* (Reception book, p. 64)
- creeping or slow walking: *Dormy, dormy dormouse* (p. 84), *Sleep, baby sleep* (Reception book, p. 36)
- swaying or swinging: *Row, row, row the boat* (Reception book, p. 63)
- jogging: *Polly, put the kettle on* (pp. 82–83), *Cobbler, cobbler* (pp. 84–85)

Use these songs to give the children opportunities to recognize different speeds or *tempi*. When they are well known, play extracts to challenge the class into responding and adjusting to the new tempo.

Listening and responding

Music for listening and moving:

- Haydn: Symphony No. 94 ('The Surprise'), 2nd movement – walking in a sprightly manner.

- Mendelssohn: Overture to *A Midsummer Night's Dream* – jogging/running lightly.

Assessment points

◆ How freely do the children move in space, finding different directions?

◆ Who can keep a steady walking beat, or jog steadily in a measured, even way?

◆ How swiftly do the children adjust from one movement to another?

Cross-curricular links

Drama, dance, PE: different types of movement, at different speeds; use of space

General learning

Speed of reaction

Musical learning

Tempo:

walking ♩

jogging ♫

slow walking ♩

Percussion instruments: long, medium and short note-durations

26 Just like me
Development lesson

Listening and responding

Remind children of the song, and the different types of moving which have been practised.

Ask them to STOP, LISTEN and THINK when hearing the first bar of the music, in order to decide which movement to do.

Listening, playing, moving

Now start to focus on two contrasting movements: walking and jogging. Whether or not one is a seasoned pianist, it is a good idea to underline the different note durations by using percussion instruments with contrasting tone qualities.

First, use a hand-held drum or tambour for 'walking' notes. Use the words 'walk, walk, walk, walk' or 'taa, taa, taa, taa' for the steady ♩ beat. Give children turns at playing the instrument.

Work on this before introducing the next idea: jogging.

Chant 'jogging, jogging, jogging, jogging' or 'ta-te ta-te ta-te ta-te' for the ♫ which will be double the speed of the ♩

Use the contrasting tone colour of wood blocks or rhythm sticks to reinforce the difference. Play a game with the children, alternating between the two. Remind them of the need to STOP, LISTEN and THINK as soon as they hear a change.

After consolidating these two speeds, introduce a third – the slow walk or 'taa-aa' ♩ preferably on a suspended cymbal with felt beater, as it produces a sustained sound.

Eventually, individual children will be able to play 'walking, jogging and slow walking' music.

Music corner activity

In the music corner, set out the three instruments used, with a workcard to encourage children to practise what they have learned.

Assessment points

◆ How quickly do children respond to change?

◆ Which children are keen to use the music corner?

27 The bear went over the mountain

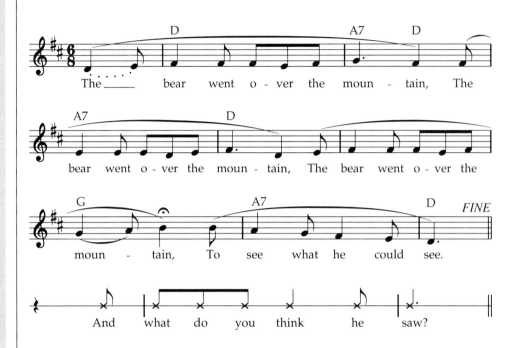

The bear went over the mountain,
The bear went over the mountain,
The bear went over the mountain,
To see what he could see.
(*spoken*) And what do you think he saw?

The other side of the mountain,
The other side of the mountain,
The other side of the mountain
(*spoken*) And what do you think he did?

So the bear went over the mountain,
The bear went over the mountain,
The bear went over the mountain,
So very happily.

Listening and singing

Discuss how this song should be sung – lightly, heavily, softly, loudly?

Use hand and arm gestures to point up the third line of the song as you teach it, pausing on the highest note before bringing it down again.

Singing and moving

In a large space, join hands in a line, pretending to be the bear going up and over the mountain, then turning round to look at it, before coming back over the mountain again. When the spoken part arrives stand on the spot and clap hands in time with the steady beat. Practise this until reasonably well co-ordinated.

Instrumental extension

Ask individual children to beat the steady beat on an untuned percussion instrument. You may like to use the piano accompaniment printed on page 87.

Now take a tuned percussion instrument such as an alto glockenspiel or xylophone, and play the ascending and descending scale to describe going up the mountain and down again. Ask the children to show with their arms upward and downward movements to match yours. Rehearse this as an introduction to the song.

*Cross-curricular
links*

Dance

General learning

*Co-operation (in
dance)*

Assessment points

◆ Can the children walk rhythmically in a line?

◆ Can they clap in time?

◆ How many can recognize upward and downward movement on a tuned percussion instrument?

Musical learning

Expression: choosing
instruments (with
awareness of register,
tone colour) and
playing styles
(including dynamics)
to represent different
animals

Improvising and
inventing

Cross-curricular
links

Science: animals and
how they move

Dance/drama: free
expression, expressive
movements
representing animals

General learning

Imaginative response

Individual
exploration

28 The bear went over the mountain
Development lesson

Variation

Ask the children to think of other animals who might go over the mountain – a squirrel, perhaps? If so, how would we sing the song – softly, lightly? How would we alter the tune to make the words fit?

Then think about the ascending and descending scale. How would it be played for a squirrel? You could suggest a lighter touch, playing the notes faster, perhaps jumping from note to note in a springy ♩ ♪ rhythm.

Instrumental extension

Develop this to explore, discuss and select tuned instruments with different registers which could represent a frog, a rabbit and an elephant – for example, a soprano glockenspiel, an alto xylophone and a bass xylophone or bass bar.

Improvising and moving

Invite three individuals to play frog, rabbit and elephant music in turn, as the rest of the class moves to the music.

Then, in small designated groups labelled frogs, rabbits, and elephants, ask one child to play an instrument making up an animal piece for the group to dance to. Ensure that turns are taken.

Music corner: playing and inventing

In the music corner, put out a set of six chime bars   D E F♯ G A B
or   C D E F G A

On a workcard, invite the children either to try to pick out parts of the tune of *The bear went over the mountain* (perhaps the last six notes), or to make up a tune of their own.

Assessment points

◆ How imaginatively do the children respond to the overall class work?

◆ Can most children sing softly, lightly, loudly, etc?

◆ Can some children make up a tune from six notes?

◆ How many can play a fragment of the tune by ear?

29 *Who made the pie?*

Music: DT

Who made the pie?   I did.   Who stole the pie?   He— did.

Who found the pie?   She did.   Who ate the pie? We *all* did.

> Who made the pie?
> > I did.
>
> Who stole the pie?
> > He did.
>
> Who found the pie?
> > She did.
>
> Who ate the pie?
> > We *all* did.

Listening and singing

This is another 'caught rather than taught' song, taken initially at a fairly slow pace. Use actions and gestures to point up the answering two-bar phrase.

Ask the children to match first the *tone* of your voice – funny, growly, light, etc. – then the *softness* or *loudness* of your voice, and finally the gradual crescendo from beginning to end.

Without singing yourself, ask the children to try to sing it all by themselves.

Conducting and singing

Then divide them into two halves, one to question, the other to answer.

Choose an individual to conduct, bringing in each group of singers at the right time. Give others a turn.

Then choose conductors to conduct with gestures for louder or softer (raising hands with palms upwards for louder, palms going down for softer).

Assessment points

◆ How quickly is the song caught?

◆ Can they match your voice, get louder and softer?

◆ Can they conduct other children?

Structure: question-and-answer

Singing: control of tone and dynamics; singing in 2 parts

Conducting, awareness of structure and dynamics

General learning

Leading (conducting), and being part of a group

30 Who made the pie?
Development lesson

Musical learning

Internalizing the rhythm of the song

Inventing rhythms for words

Observing and responding to changes of tempo and dynamics

Musical conversations with body-sounds and instruments

Internalizing the song

Sing the song again as a class.

Then ask the children to think the song in their heads, while you clap the question and they clap the answer. Change round so that the class starts. Try alternatives to clapping: tapping, etc.

A question-and-answer game

Arrange the children in a circle. Go right round the circle asking, in a rhythmical manner, 'What is your name?', leaving a gap for the answer. Then encourage the children to ask you the same question in return.

Extend this activity to other questions, for instance: 'What did you have for supper last night?'

Once this idea has been grasped, go back to 'What is your name? – but this time, as well as asking the question, simultaneously clap it (one clap with each syllable, keeping the whole thing rhythmic). Encourage a similar style of response – the child's name, spoken plus clapped.

This game can be varied in a number of ways. The children may enjoy it if you vary the tempo, asking the questions fast or slow and expecting a similar response.

Further possible variations include:
> quiet questions – quiet answers
> loud questions – loud answers

or opposites:
> quiet questions – loud answers, etc.

Musical conversations

Return to the rhythm patterns of the song. Clap the rhythm of 'Who made the pie?', then tap the rhythm of 'I did'. Do the children recognize what you are doing?

Take an untuned percussion instrument for yourself, and give a different one to an individual child. Perform the same two lines, using the two instruments to make the question and the answer:

Give other children a turn. Then show how you can continue to have a musical conversation using instruments.

Arrange the children in pairs and give them time to explore the possibilities of musical conversations. Clapping or tapping can substitute for instruments, but ensure that everyone has a turn with an instrument.

This activity can also be transferred to the music corner.

Assessment points

◆ How responsive is the class to this activity?

◆ Can the children match syllables with sound?

◆ How well can most children transfer this activity to instruments?

31 Stars

Slowly and softly

It's grow-ing dark, the_ stars are_ twink-ling.

Close your eyes and_ gent - ly sleep,

Gent - ly sleep, gent - ly_ sleep.

It's growing dark, the stars are twinkling.
Close your eyes and gently sleep,
Gently sleep, gently sleep.

Listening, responding, understanding

Ask the children to listen carefully to the music and do what the words say. Sing the song without any accompaniment – slowly, softly, smoothly.

How many children actually closed their eyes? Ask them what they heard (your voice singing).

Now sing the song again, this time asking the children to close their eyes *before* you start.

Ask them what the song is about, and what it is for. Discuss with them the nature of a lullaby.

Musical learning

Feeling for a lullaby

♩ ♩ ♩

rhythm pattern

*Expression:
sound qualities of
different percussion
instruments*

Rhythmic movement

Listening, moving, singing

Ask the children to sway gently in time as you sing. Afterwards, whisper and sway to the following pattern:

gent - ly sleep,   gent - ly sleep

Ask the children to join in. Point out the difference between whispering and singing.

Then sing the song again, asking the children to join in with the last four bars ('Close your eyes ...') as they absorb the song. Note that this is a lullaby to be absorbed (caught rather than taught) as new ideas are introduced into each repetition.

Ensure that the spirit (expressive quality) of the music is learned by vocalizing to 'loo' or 'la'.

Finally, teach the whole song, if necessary taking the words phrase by phrase (always with the melody line).

Adding instruments

After patting out the 'gently sleep' rhythm on legs or thighs, repeat it on Indian bells, triangle or suspended cymbal while the children pat or clap the rhythm.

gent - ly sleep

Try out different instruments to achieve a variety of effects, inviting individual children to describe the sound qualities, e.g. twinkling, shining, bright, etc.

Assessment points

◆ Which children are quick to join in? (Give help – additional cues, eye contact, visual aids – to those who are not.)

◆ Which children are readily grasping songs (rhythm and pitch)?

◆ How many children can pat correctly the 'gently sleep' rhythm?

Cross-curricular links

Language: vocabulary, enunciation, comprehension

General learning

Concentration when listening

Articulating ideas

Musical learning

rhythm pattern

Timbre: recognition of instruments

Exploring sounds: by dynamics, by expressive quality

Rhythmic movement

Listening: Dohnányi's Variations on a Nursery Theme

32 Stars
Development lesson

Go over the lullaby *Stars*

A matching game

Give yourself a set of several instruments, and the children an identical set. Sit in a circle with the children.

Isolate the 'gently sleep' pattern, saying it as you play:

gent - ly   sleep

Ask children in turn to match the 'gently sleep' pattern, first by trying to play it at the same time, then by playing it immediately after you.

Take time with this, giving individuals space and flexibility to explore and practise this skill.

If you have a screen or other suitable piece of furniture, play a guessing game in which children, in turn, hide behind the screen and choose an instrument for the other children to identify when played.

Music corner activity

Arrange a selection of suitable instruments with workcards for exploring, investigating, and comparing sounds. For example:
    'Can you play soft sounds?'
    'Can you play twinkling sounds?'
    'Can you play ringing sounds?'

Singing

Here is another song about stars:

Twinkle, twinkle little star

Twinkle, twinkle little star,
How I wonder what you are.
Up above the world so high,
Like a diamond in the sky.
Twinkle, twinkle little star,
How I wonder what you are.

Responding through movement

Ask the children to pat the walking rhythm gently on their thighs. Then invite them to tip-toe round the hall in time with the music.

Listening

Listen to an extract from *Variations on a Nursery Theme* by Dohnányi. Do the children recognize the theme?

Prepare the children to move to the music until they hear the *Twinkle, twinkle* theme, which is a signal to sit down and listen.

Cross-curricular links

English: reading workcards

General learning

Concentration when listening

Working as a class, and as an individual

Investigating (sound corner activities)

Assessment points

◆ Record achievement in matching the 'gently sleep' rhythm.

◆ Note children who are interested in using the sound corner.

◆ How many children made an instant response to the entry of the *Twinkle, twinkle* theme?

33 Cats and dogs

Musical learning

Vocal skills: singing and chanting, singing expressively (varying speed and weight), exploring and performing word-sounds

Co-ordination in performance: different actions with different vocal styles

Rhythm patterns

Pitch/tonality: internalizing and memorizing a starting note

Improvising

Cats

Words: Eleanor Farjeon
Music: DT

Cats sleep	Anybody's
Anywhere,	Lap will do,
Any table,	Fitted in a
Any chair,	Cardboard box,
Top of piano,	In the cupboard
Window-ledge,	With your frocks –
In the middle,	Anywhere!
On the edge,	*They* don't care!
Open drawer,	Cats sleep
Empty shoe,	Anywhere.

Listening and performing

This piece goes alternately from song to chant. Teach it as if all the words are chanted before teaching it as written. Sing confidently, and chant the spoken phrases in a stage whisper.

Clap the rhythm as you and the children sing. *Tap* the rhythm as you all chant.

Help the children to remember the pitch of the starting note, which is always the same: G.

My puppy

Words: Aileen Fisher
Music: DT

Moderate speed

It's fun - ny my pup - py knows just how I feel. When I'm

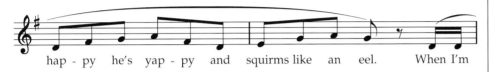

hap - py he's yap - py and squirms like an eel. When I'm

slower

grum - py he's slum - py and stays at my heel. It's

Tempo I

fun - ny my pup - py knows such a great deal.

It's funny
my puppy
knows just how I feel.

When I'm happy
he's yappy
and squirms like an eel.

When I'm grumpy
he's slumpy
and stays at my heel.

It's funny
my puppy
knows such a great deal.

Listening and performing

Teach this song in a similar way.

It deals in contrasts of speed and weight. The third line needs to be sung slowly and heavily; the other three lightly.

Assessment points

◆ How well do the children alternate clapping and tapping?

◆ How rhythmically do the children sing both songs?

Language: two poems, vocabulary, enunciation

General learning

Quick and flexible response

Musical learning

Pitch relationships

Creating pitch
patterns

Rhythm patterns

Internalizing

34 Cats and dogs
Development lesson

Pitch games

Sol-fa syllables are printed above the music of *Cats*. They provide a tangible means of relating different pitches to each other, helping to fix these relationships (rather like number bonds, which link the 'ten-ness' of 5 + 5, 6 + 4, 7 + 3, etc.).

These little games are useful for focusing on pitch relationships and for improving intonation. Using hand signs, teach the children to follow your lead:

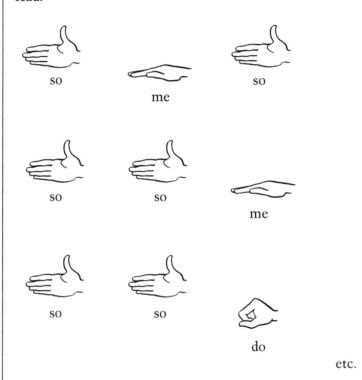

etc.

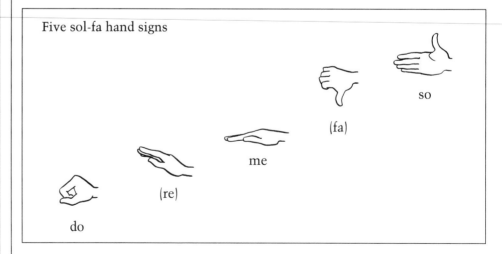

Five sol-fa hand signs

See how many different three-note patterns can be made from do, me and so.

Rhythm games

Remind the children of the rhythms of *Cats* and *My puppy*. Clap or pat them.

Then tap out on the table, or with rhythm sticks, isolated, characterful phrases for the children to guess which song they come from, e.g.:

Ask if anyone can think and clap the beginning of *Cats*; then ask for another volunteer for *My puppy*.

In a circle, see if one of the songs can be taken all round the class, phrase by phrase, singing and clapping at the same time. Then introduce the challenge of *clapping* each phrase while *silently thinking* the words.

Finally equip each child with an untuned percussion instrument, and go round the circle playing each phrase of the song in turn.

Vocal improvising

Highlight the consonants used in *My puppy*. Play with them. Use some of them to make short rhythm phrases, for instance:

f ———— p j   (long–short–short)

h h h   (three short sounds)

Assessment points

◆ How quickly do the children pick up the hand signs?

◆ How well can they pitch the sol-fa syllables?

◆ Who is keen to make up three-note patterns?

◆ Which children can guess the tune from the rhythm?

◆ How many children show fluency and ready response when song
   phrases are: a) sung and clapped?
                 b) thought and clapped?
                 c) played?

Cross-curricular links

Language: exploring consonants

General learning

Co-ordination and co-operation in circle games

35 Little frog

Musical learning

Singing technique: long phrases; expressiveness

1. Oh the little frog sat sighing on a lily pond one day,
   Oh the little frog sat sighing on a lily pond one day.
   I'm sighing for a play-mate, I'm sighing for a play-mate,
   I'm sighing for a play-mate, on this fine day.

2. Oh the little frog sat waiting on a lily pond one day,
   Oh the little frog sat waiting on a lily pond one day.
   I'll croak for a playmate, I'll croak for a playmate,
   I'll croak for a playmate, on this fine day.

   Croak, croak, croak, croak, croak   *(getting louder)*

Listening and performing

This is another song to be 'caught rather than taught'.

Concentrate here on setting a steady, easy tempo. Try to encourage long phrases, with control of breathing and good articulation.

3. Oh _ two frogs sat laugh-ing on a li-ly pond one

day, Oh two frogs sat laugh-ing on a li-ly pond one

day. They are laugh-ing till their sides ache, They are laugh-ing till their

sides ache, They are laugh-ing till their sides ache on this fine day.

3. Oh two frogs sat laughing on a lily pond one day,
   Oh two frogs sat laughing on a lily pond one day.
   They are laughing, till their sides ache, they are laughing till their
      sides ache,
   They are laughing till their sides ache, on this fine day.

   Croak, croak, croak, croak, croak, croak, CROAK, CROAK.

Act the story out. It can be taken beyond three verses – adding more frogs, and with frogs hopping around as they croak and croak.

Suggest to the children that they use an instrument to amplify the croaking sound (ideally a guiro).

Assessment points

◆ How quickly is the song learned?

◆ Are most of the children able to maintain the phrase without running out of air?

◆ Are the children good at passing on instruments to enable full participation?

36 Little frog
Development lesson

Musical learning

Listening and appraising: expressive quality (happy or sad)

Tonality (major/minor)

Inventing and comparing 5-note patterns

Playing phrases from the song

Listening and discussing

Play the first verse. Ask the children how they think the music sounds. What kind of feeling or character does it have?

Respond positively to answers and move towards the notion of the sad quality of the opening verses.

Now play verse 3 ('Oh two frogs sat laughing ...'). How is this music different from verse 1? What feeling or character does it have? Is this sad music?

Inventing and investigating

Set out these chime bars:

     D   E   F   G   A

See how many patterns individual children can make out of these five notes.

Now, keeping the first set accessible, put out another set:

     D   E   F♯   G   A

Invite individuals to make patterns out of *this* set.

Is there a difference? What is the difference? Is there a difference of *feeling*?

Play matching games, and make a distinctive feature of the difference between the F and the F♯. These do not match.

Play the opening phrase of the song on each of the sets. Ask children to see if they can do the same.

Talk about sad music and happy music.

Transfer the instruments to the music corner so that children can practise in feer periods of activity.

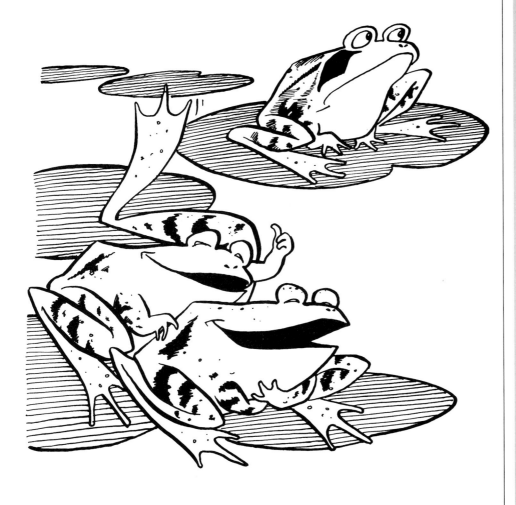

Cross-curricular
links

Language: discussion

General learning

Talking about
feelings and emotions

Assessment points

◆ How well do the children concentrate when asked to listen?

◆ How many children can match sounds?

◆ Who makes a good attempt at finding the first phrase of the song?

37 The band in the park

Musical learning

Steady marching pulse

Timing movements and body-sounds

Listening: Sousa's The Stars and Stripes forever

Words: Paul Edmonds
Music: DT

Steady speed

Hark, hark, hark, hark, hark, hark! Lis-ten to the band in the park! With its 'hum hum hum' And its 'rump-ty tump-ty tum,' The cym-bals go-ing 'clang' And the drums go-ing 'bang,' As they play, play, play, play, play, play, play, As they play, play, play, in the mid-dle of the day, As they play, play, play in the park.

Hark, hark, hark, hark, hark, hark!
Listen to the band in the park!
With its 'hum hum hum'
And its 'rumpty tumpty tum',
The cymbals going 'clang'
And the drums going 'bang',
As they play, play, play, play, play, play, play,
As they play, play, play, in the middle of the day,
As they play, play, play in the park.

Listening and performing

Teach the song, noting that there are short phrases and long phrases. Mark the steady beat when teaching to ensure a feeling for the marching quality.

Ask the children to imagine that they have instruments to play, and encourage them to act like a marching band, marching to the steady beat all the way through to the band stand.

When the song is learned, bring the children into a standing circle. This time, ask them to give a big clap when the word 'clang' is reached, similarly with the word 'bang'. Next, invite them to clap on every word 'play', and also on the three words at the end – 'in the park'.

Instrumental extension

Ask for two volunteers to stand in the centre of the circle. Give one a pair of cymbals or a suspended cymbal, and the other a drum. While the rest of the class marches on the spot to the steady beat, the two soloists play their cymbal and drum at the relevant points in the song. Invite other children to take turns.

Listening and moving

Play the Sousa march *The Stars and Stripes forever*, and invite the class to move freely to the music.

Cross-curricular links

Language: onomatopoeic words

Dance/drama: mime

General learning

Co-ordination

Taking turns

Assessment points

◆ Can the majority of children keep a steady beat when marching?

◆ Can most children manage to sing while moving?

◆ Note children who need a lot of preparation in order to be ready with their 'clangs' and 'bangs'.

38 The band in the park
Development lesson

Musical learning

Dynamics: controlled crescendo

Steady marching pulse

Structure

Improvisation: exploring percussion instruments and their tone colour

Performing

Review the song, and encourage the children to imagine a band getting nearer and nearer. How should we start the song? Really softly? Should we get *suddenly* louder or *gradually* louder?

Next, draw the children into a circle. Sing the song, asking the children to start with quiet marching on the spot, getting gradually louder, matching voices with feet movements.

The next sequence helps to point up the structure of the song. Make two lines, children following a leader. Each line marches on the spot for the first four phrases of the song, up to 'going bang', when the leaders lead them round the room or hall and back to their original starting positions.

Instrumental extension

Take turns with instruments as before. Then help the children to think about adding new instruments, adding each one just after 'the cymbals going clang'. This will lengthen the song, for example: 'the shaker going jingle, the triangle going tingle ...'.

Music corner activity

Print the words of the song on a card. Put out a selection of instruments and some workcards which ask the questions:

'What kind of sound does a chime bar make? Try it and find out.'

'What kind of sound does a guiro make? Does it jingle, chime or make a scrapy sound?'

Cross-curricular links

Physical Education: rhythmical response

General learning

Imagination

Structural awareness

Assessment points

◆ How controlled are children's voices, movements and group activities?

◆ How well do the leaders lead?

◆ Do most children remember when to march on the spot and when to move?

◆ For how long do individuals concentrate in the music corner?

Father and Mother and Uncle John

(see pages 20–21)

Music: DT

This is the way the ladies ride

(see page 23)

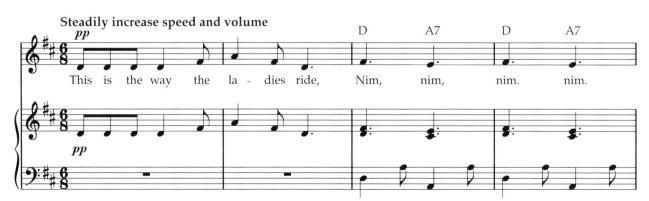

This is the way the gen-tle-men ride, Trim, trim, trim, trim. This is the way the farm - ers ride, Trot, trot, trot, trot. This is the way the hunts - men ride, A - gal-lop, a - gal-lop, a - gal-lop, a - gal-lop. This is the way the plough - boys ride, Hob ble-dy - gee, hob-ble-dy-gee, hob-ble-dy - gee. *Spoken:* And down into a DITCH!

To market, to market to buy a fat pig

(see page 22)

Music: DT

Polly, put the kettle on

(see page 55)

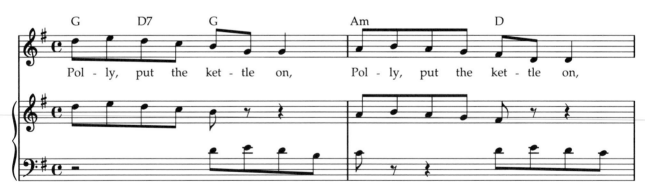

Su-key, take it off a-gain, Su-key, take it off a-gain, They've all gone a-way.

The grand old Duke of York

(see page 55)

Oh, the grand old Duke of York, He had ten thou-sand men. He

marched them up to the top of the hill And he marched them down a - gain. And

when they were up they were up, And when they were down they were down, And

when they were on - ly half - way up They were nei - ther up nor down.

Dormy, dormy dormouse

(see page 55)

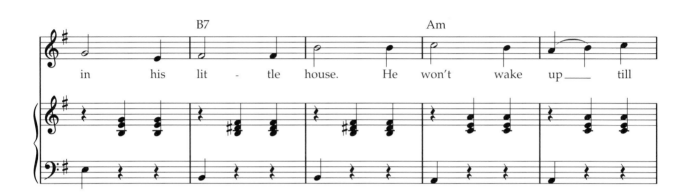

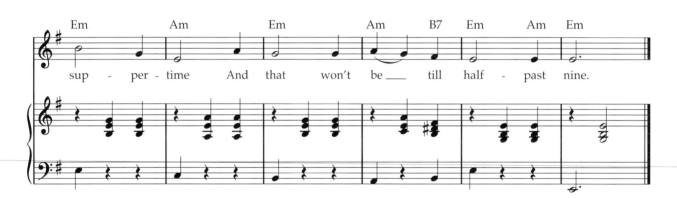

Cobbler, cobbler

(see page 55)

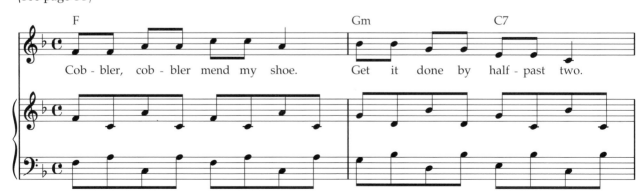

84

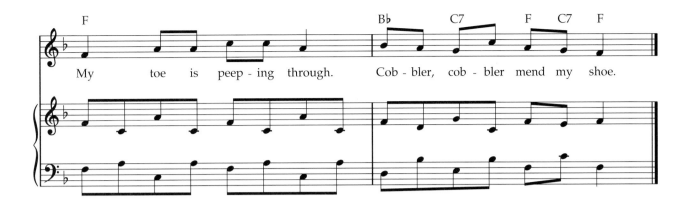

My toe is peep-ing through. Cob-bler, cob-bler mend my shoe.

London Bridge is broken down

(see page 55)

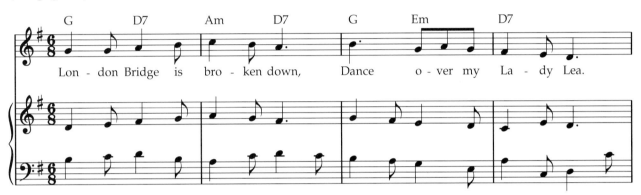

Lon - don Bridge is bro - ken down, Dance o - ver my La - dy Lea.

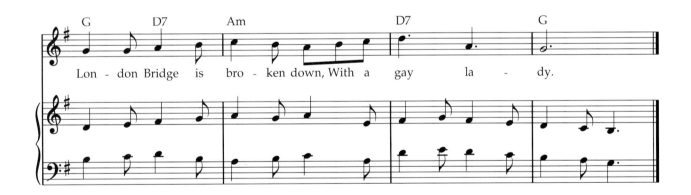

Lon - don Bridge is bro - ken down, With a gay la - dy.

2. How shall we build it up again ...

3. Build it up with silver and gold ...

4. Silver and gold will be stolen away ...

5. Build it up with iron and steel ...

6. Iron and steel will bend and break ...

7. Build it up with stone so strong ...
   Hurrah 'twill last for ages long.

Aiken Drum

(see page 55)

There __ was a man lived in the moon, lived in the moon, lived

in the moon. There was a man lived in the moon and his name was Aik - en

Drum. And he played up-on a la - dle, a la - dle, a-

la - dle, And he played up-on a la - dle, And his name was Aik - en Drum.

The bear went over the mountain

(see page 58–9)

Spoken: And what do you think he saw?

D. C. al Fine

If all the world were paper

(see page 55)

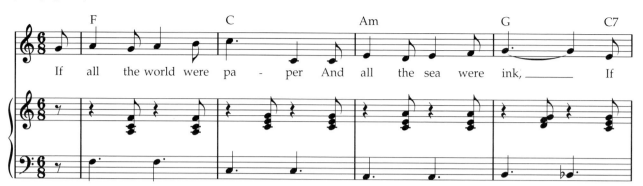

Luke's lullaby

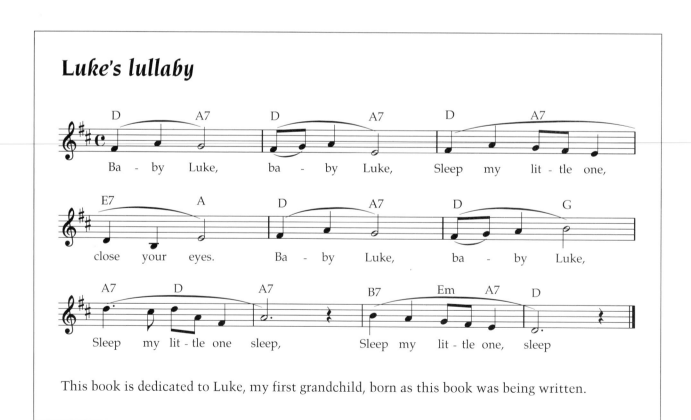

This book is dedicated to Luke, my first grandchild, born as this book was being written.